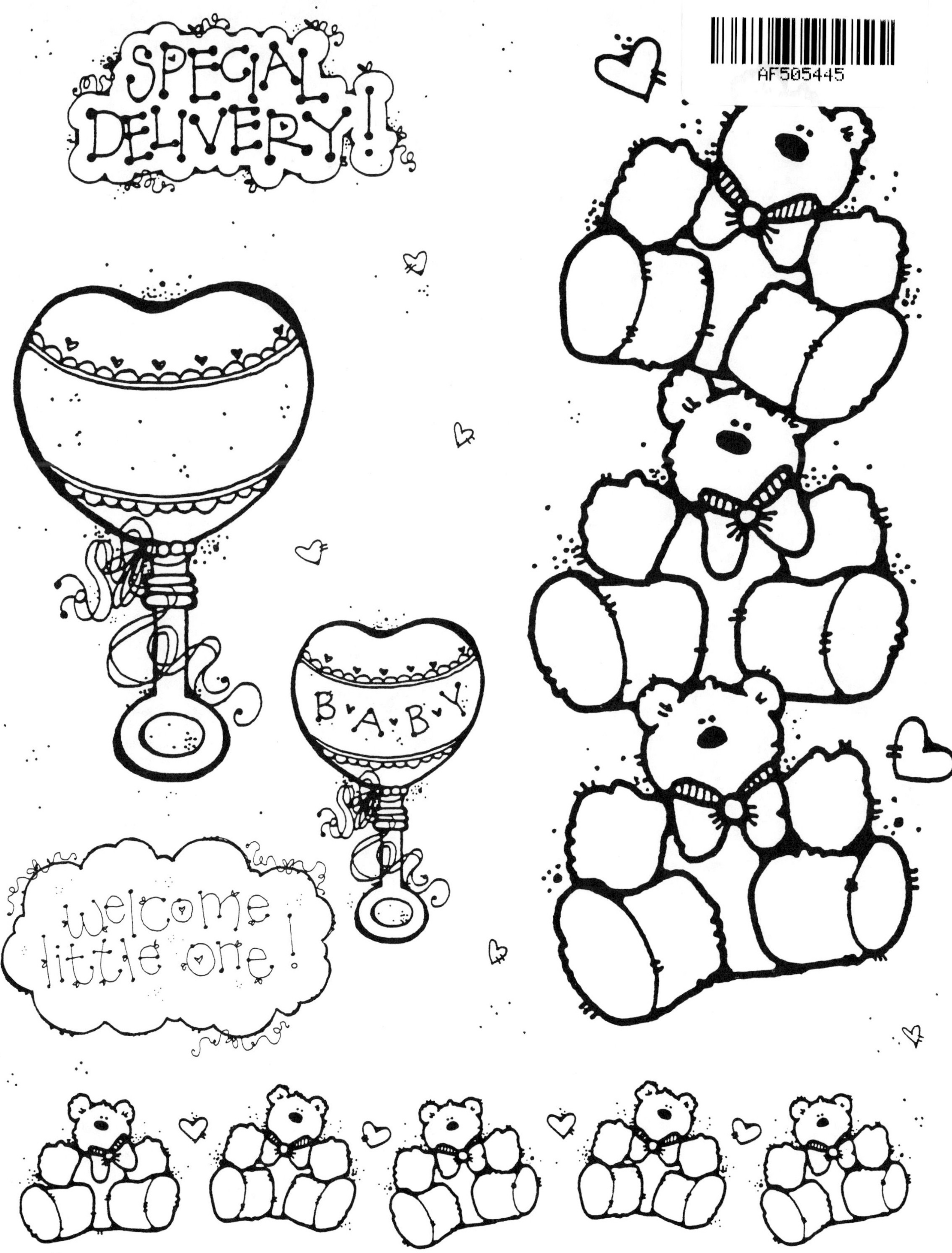

SPECIAL DELIVERY!
BABY
welcome little one!
AF505445
designs © dianne j. hook 1995

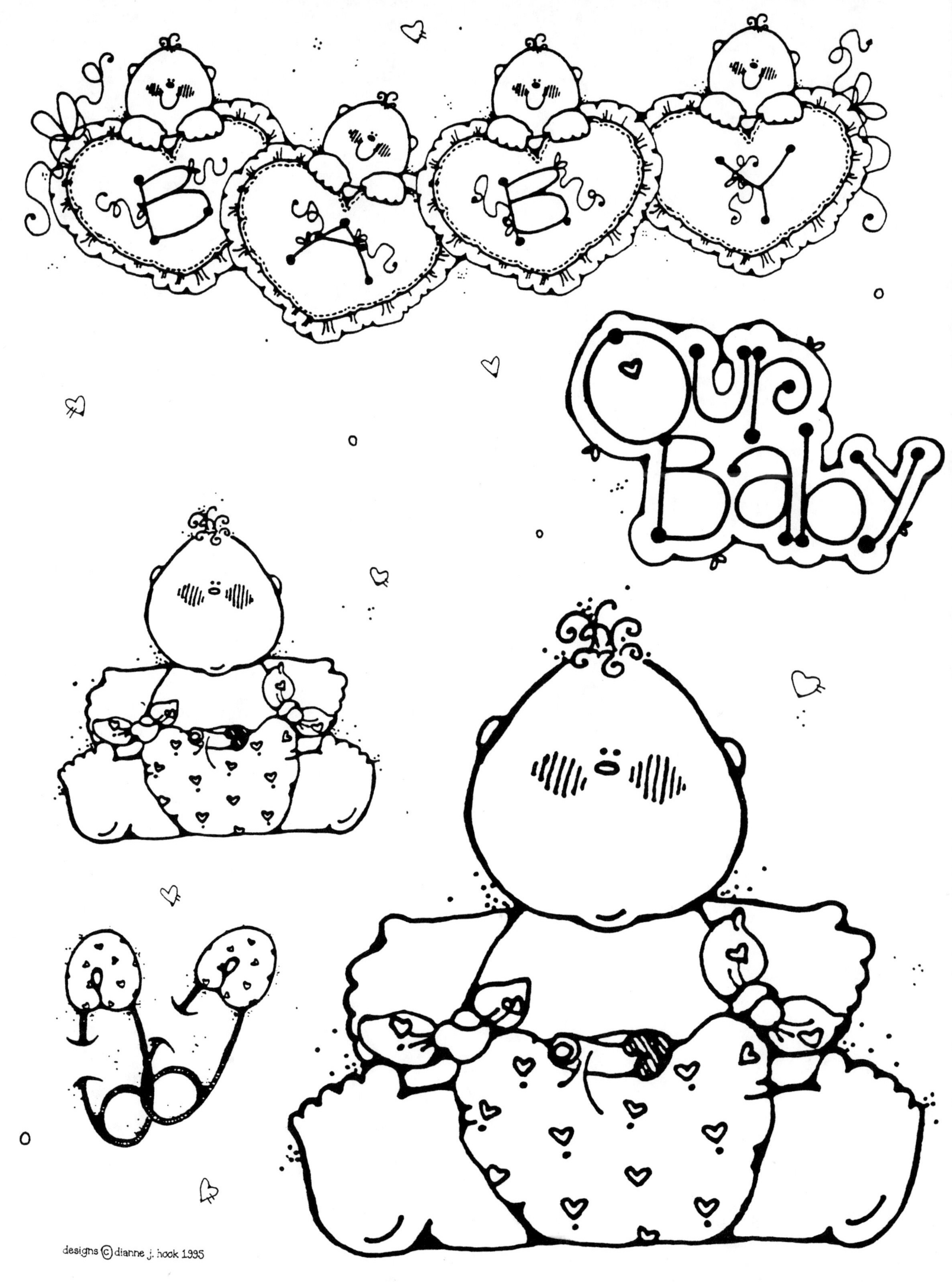

Our Baby
designs © dianne j. hook 1995

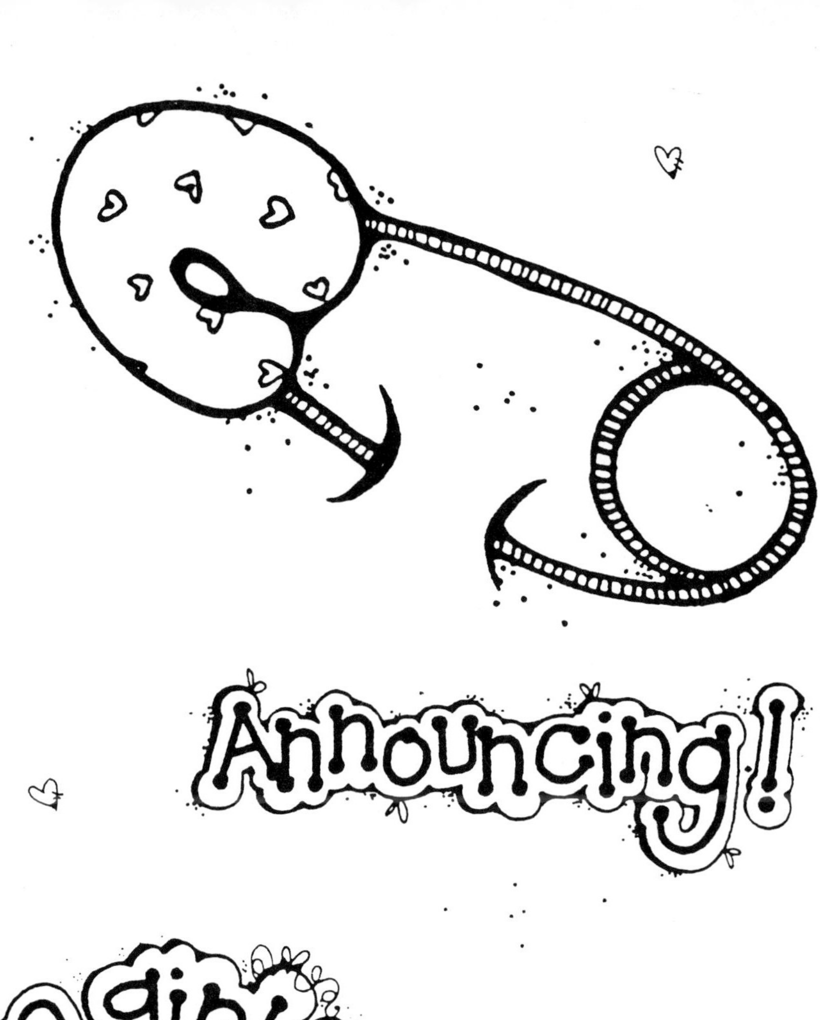

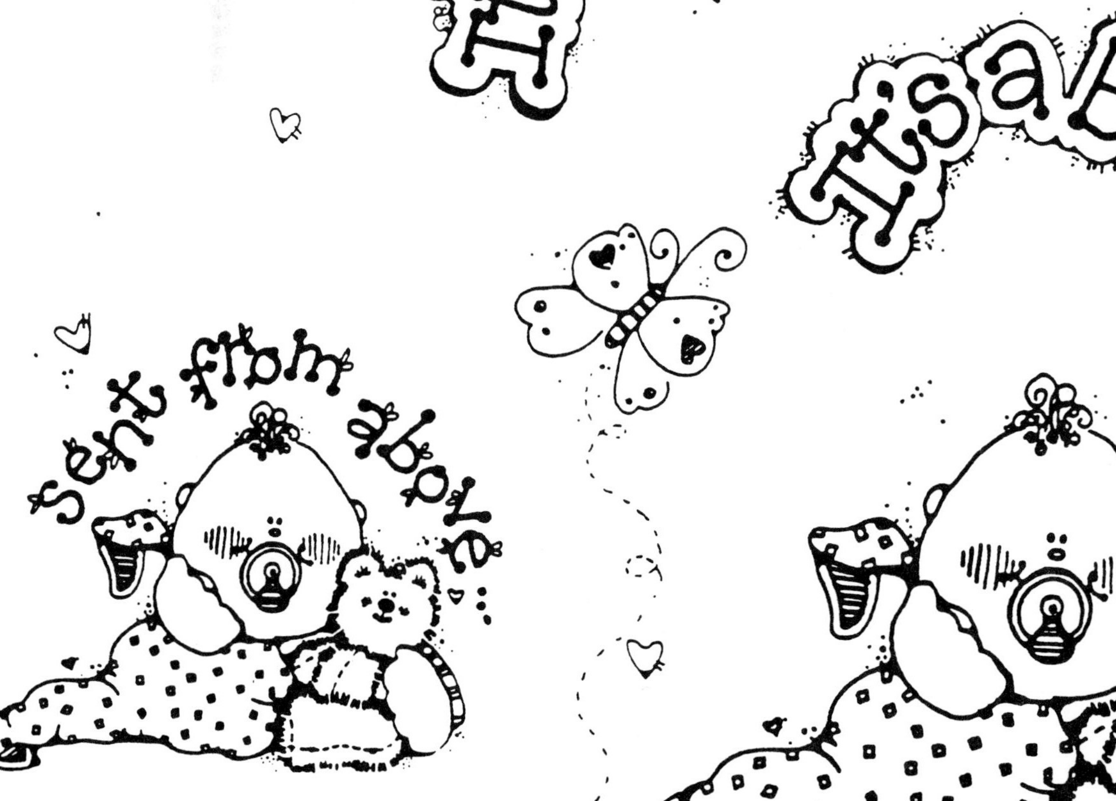

designs © dianne j. hook 1995

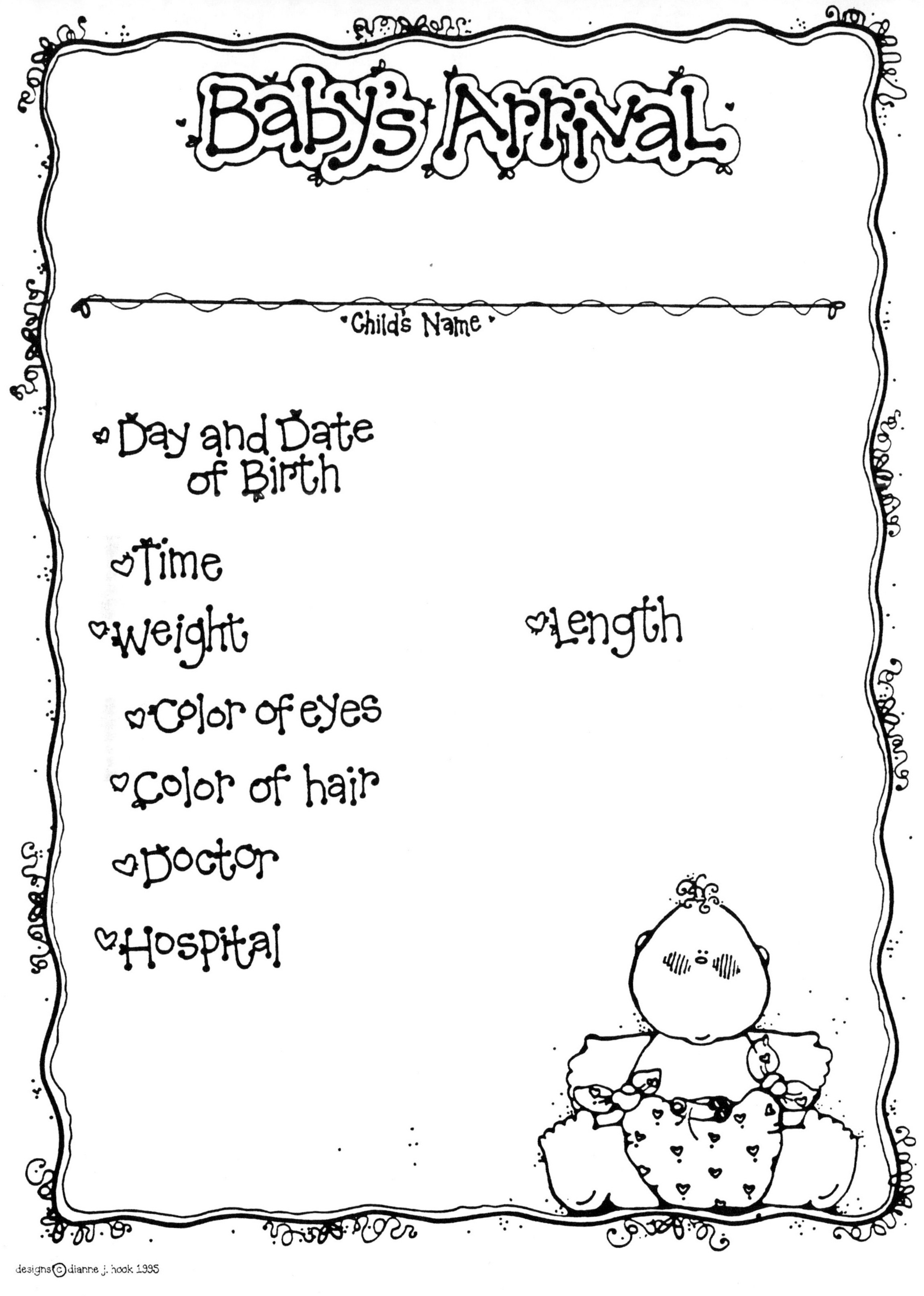

Baby's Arrival

· Child's Name ·

- Day and Date of Birth
- Time
- Weight
- Length
- Color of eyes
- Color of hair
- Doctor
- Hospital

designs © dianne j. hook 1995

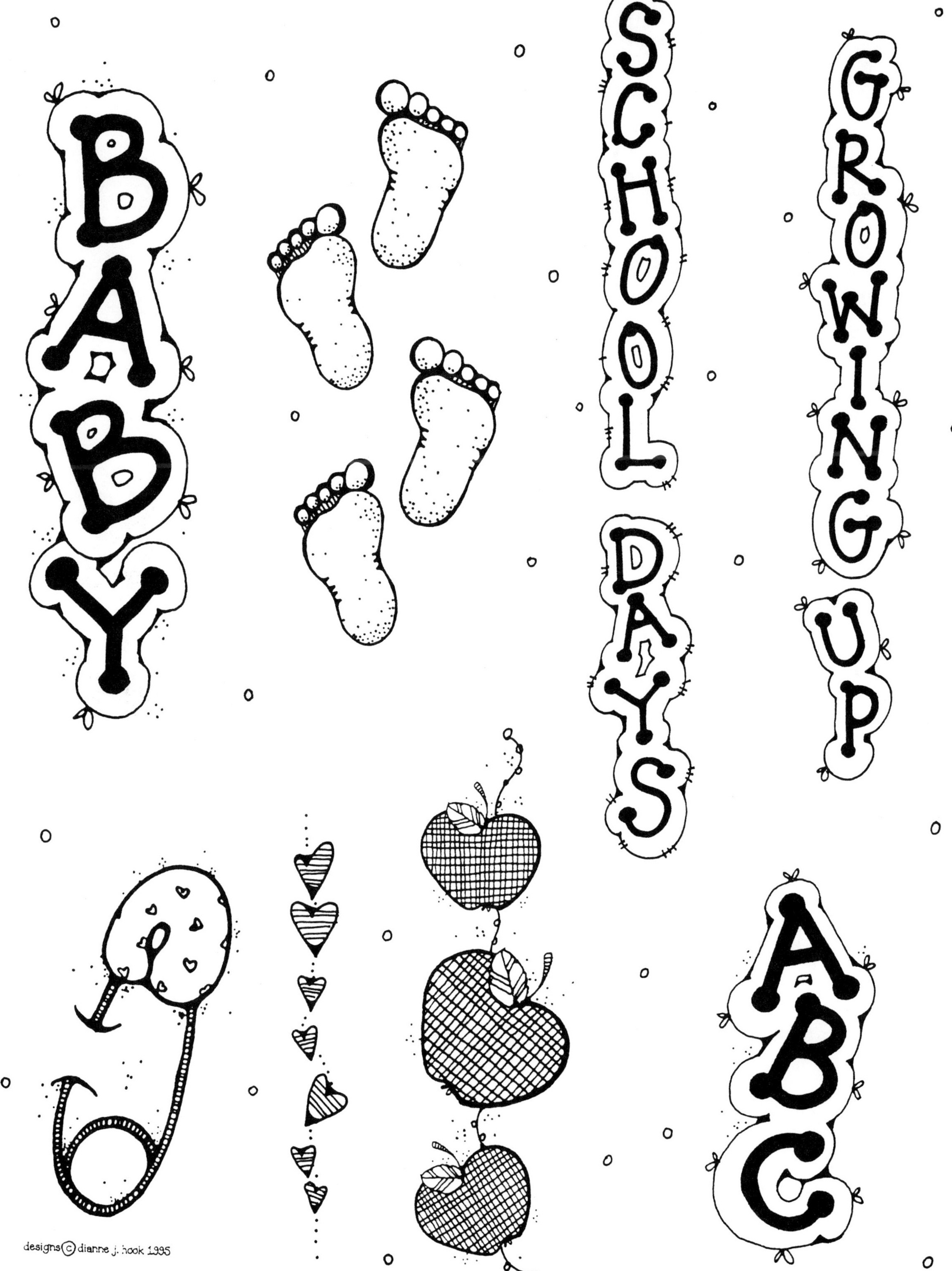

designs © dianne j. hook 1995

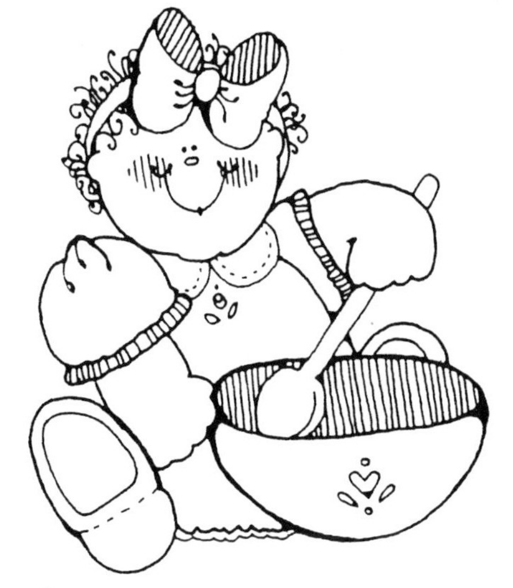

mommy's Little helper !

"Look what I made !"

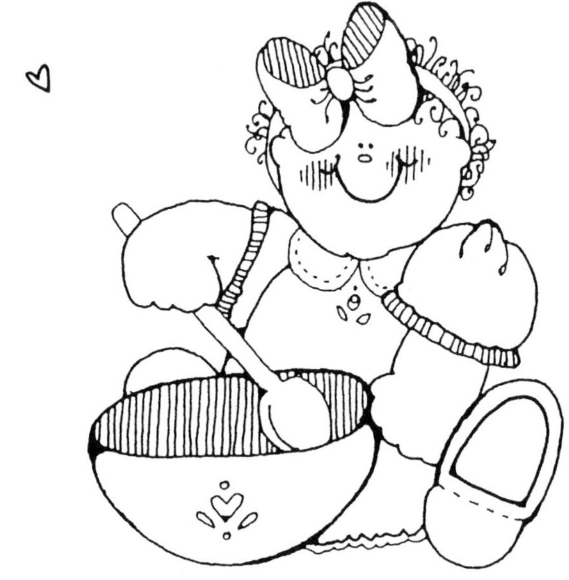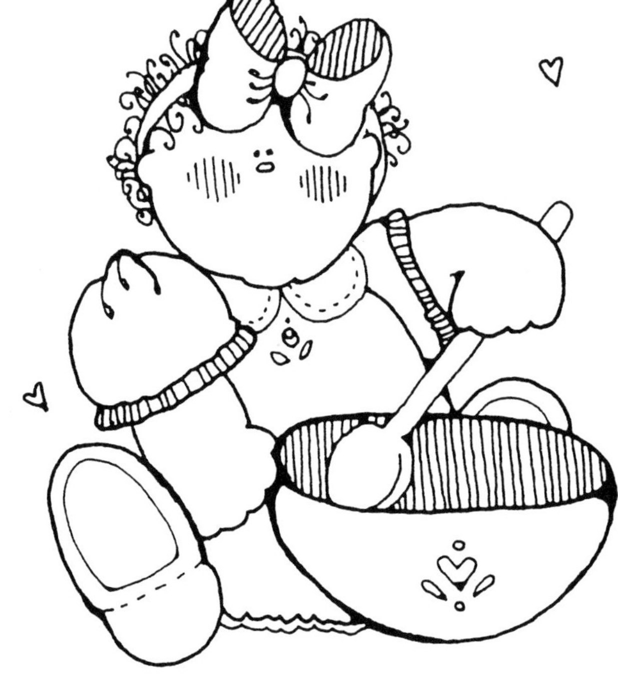

something special just for you....

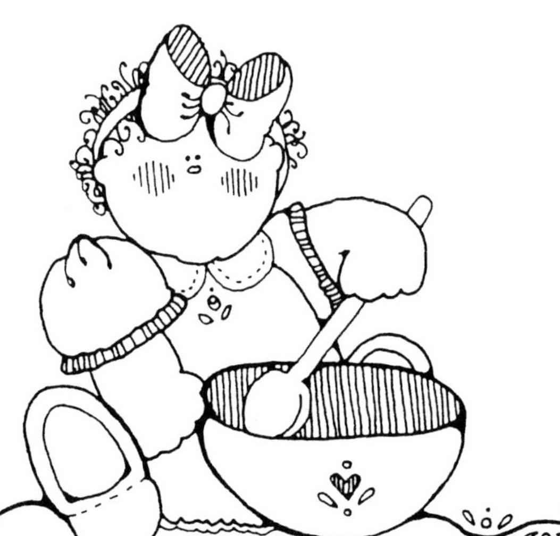

designs © dianne j. hook 1995

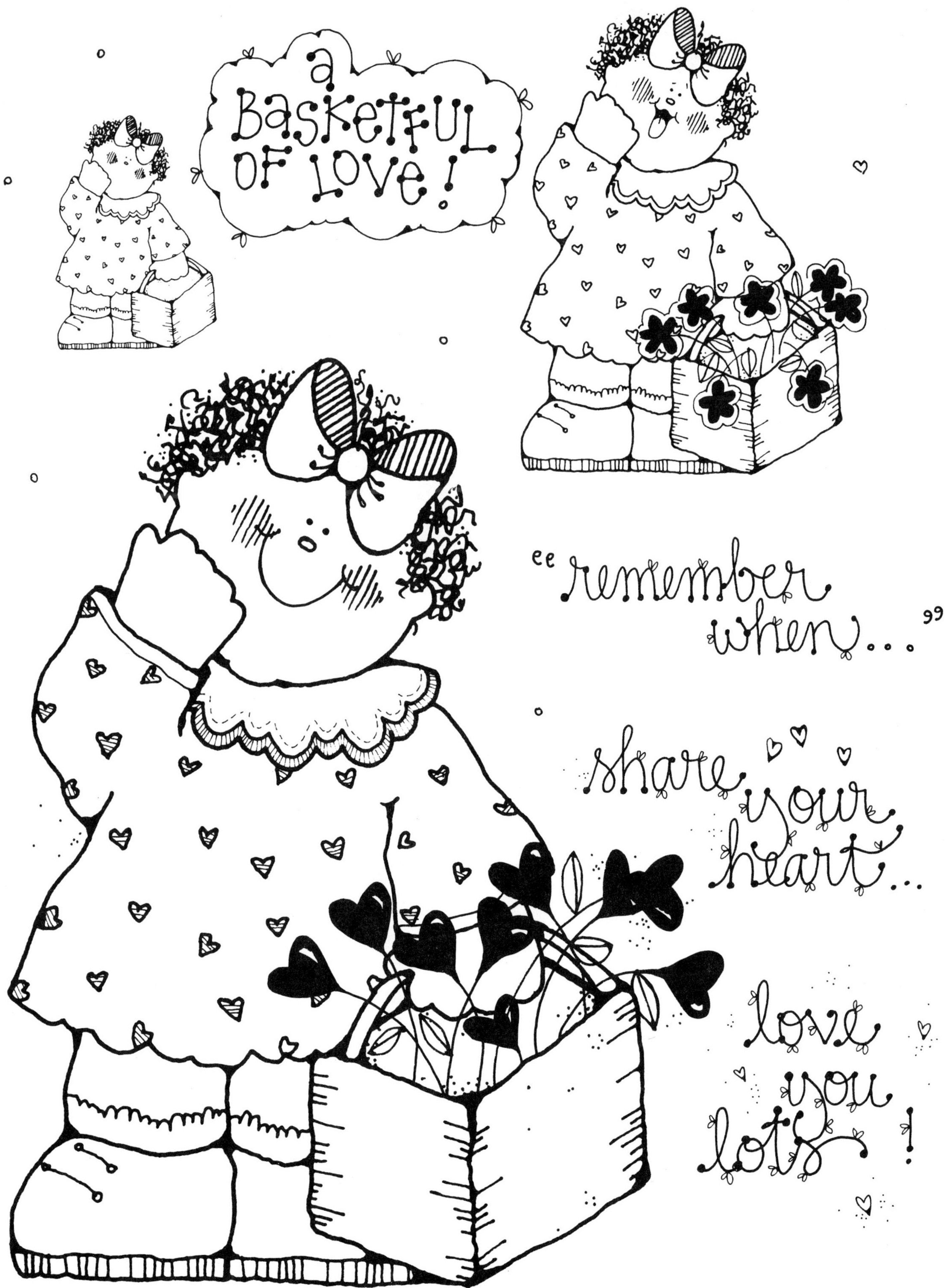

a Basketful of Love!
"remember when..."
share your heart...
love you lots!
designs © dianne j. hook 1995

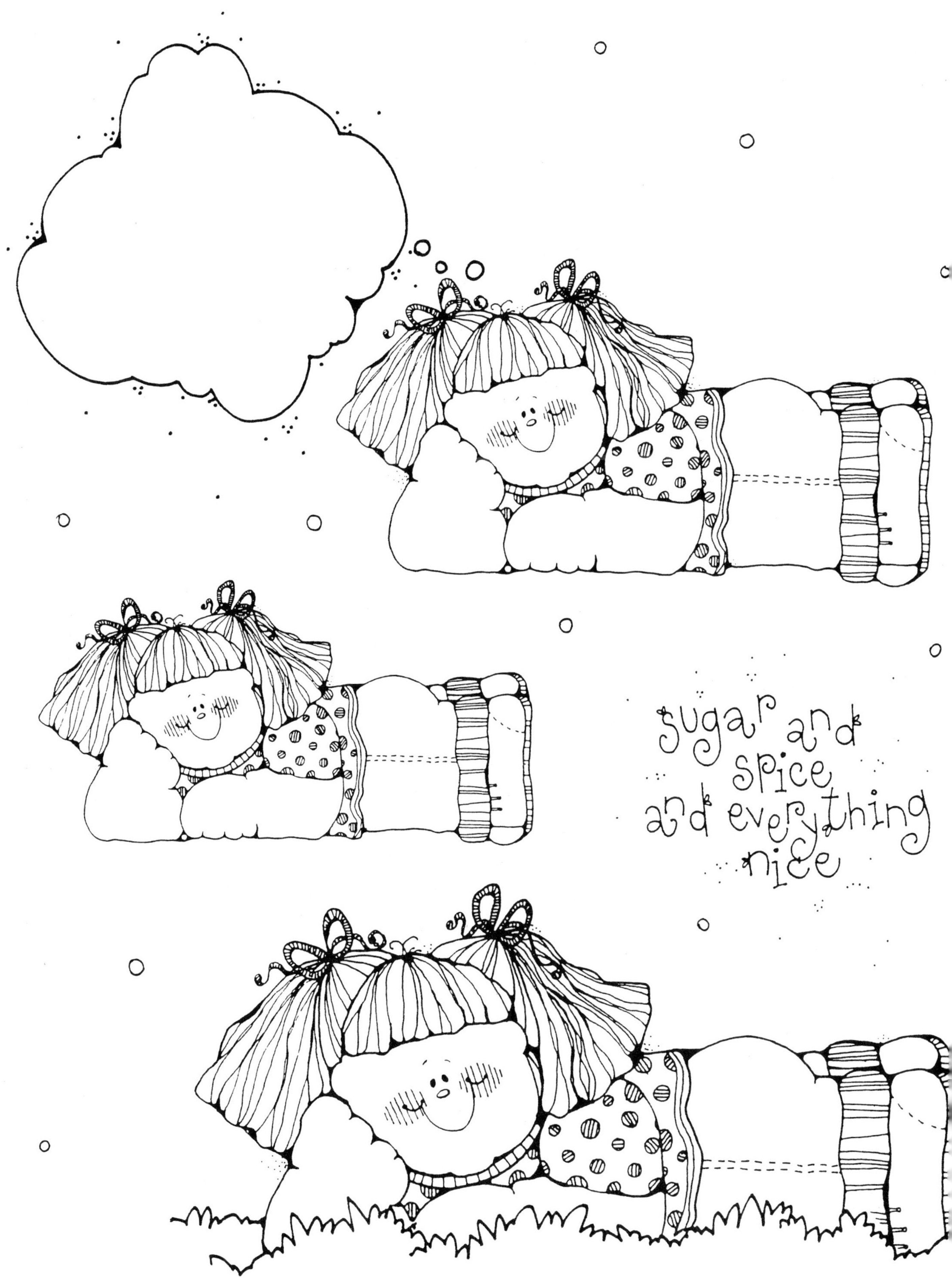

designs © dianne j. hook 1995

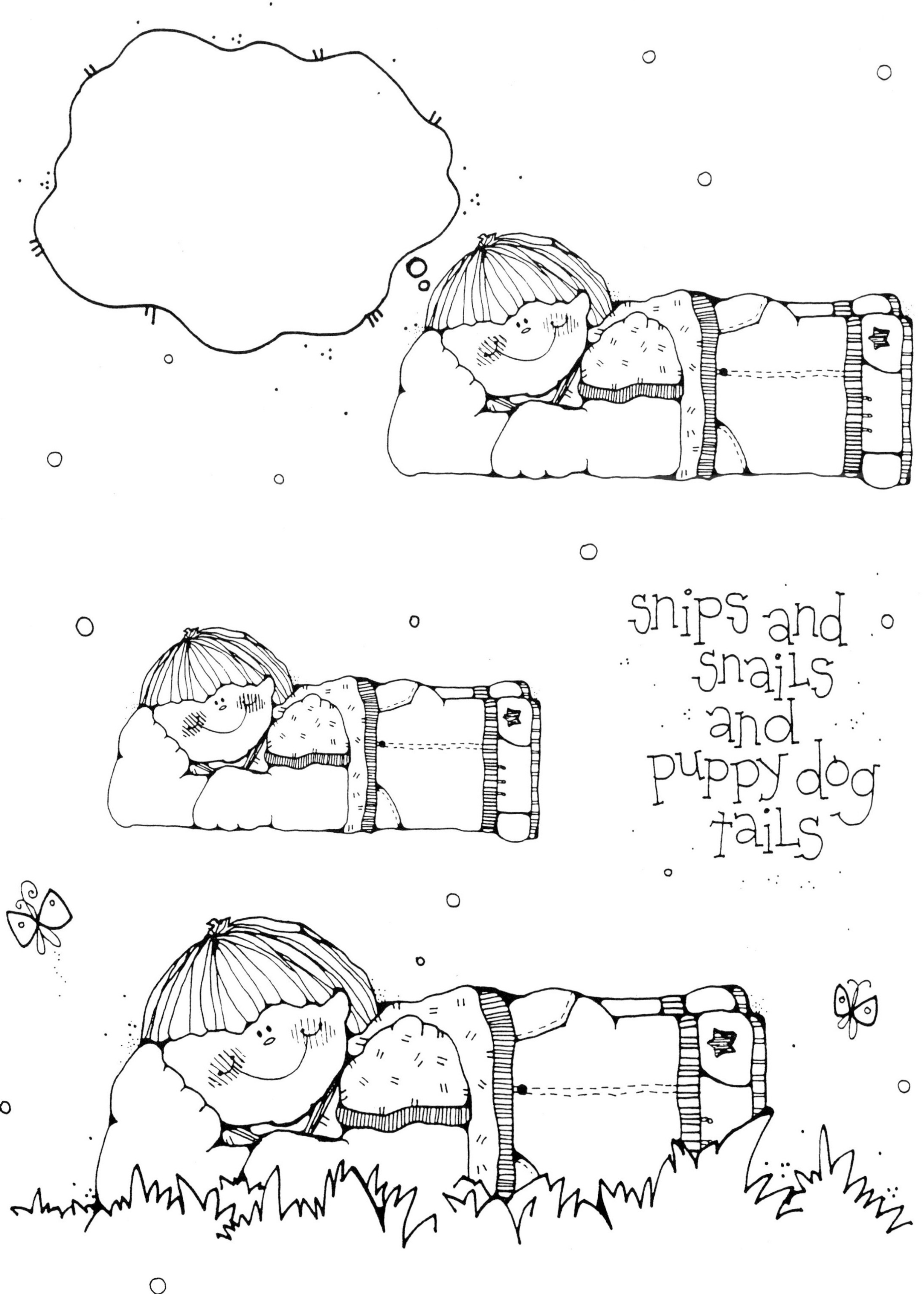

designs © dianne j. hook 1995

I'M GLAD THERE'S a YOU !
designs © dianne j. hook 1995

...MY CLASSMATES...

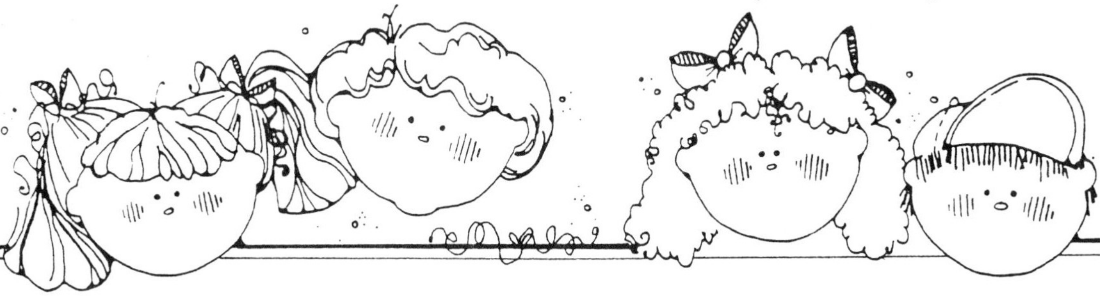

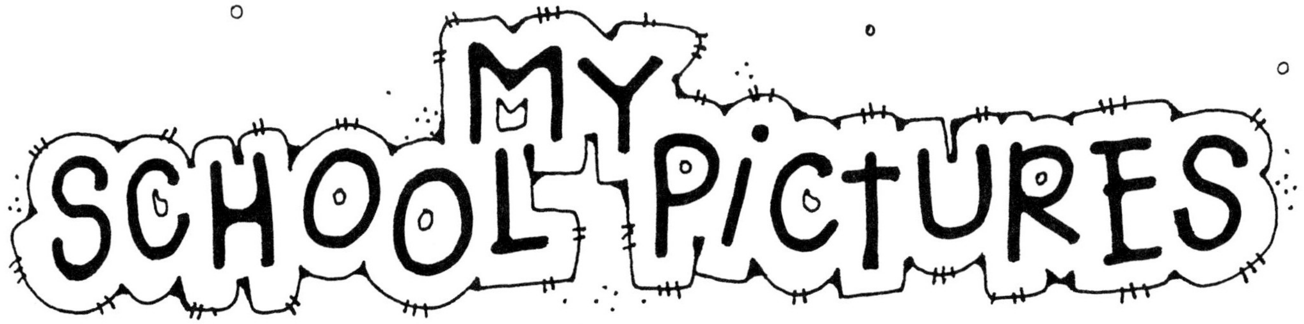

designs © dianne j. hook 1995

designs © dianne j. hook 1995

HAPPY Birthday

the best day ever !

designs © dianne j. hook 1995

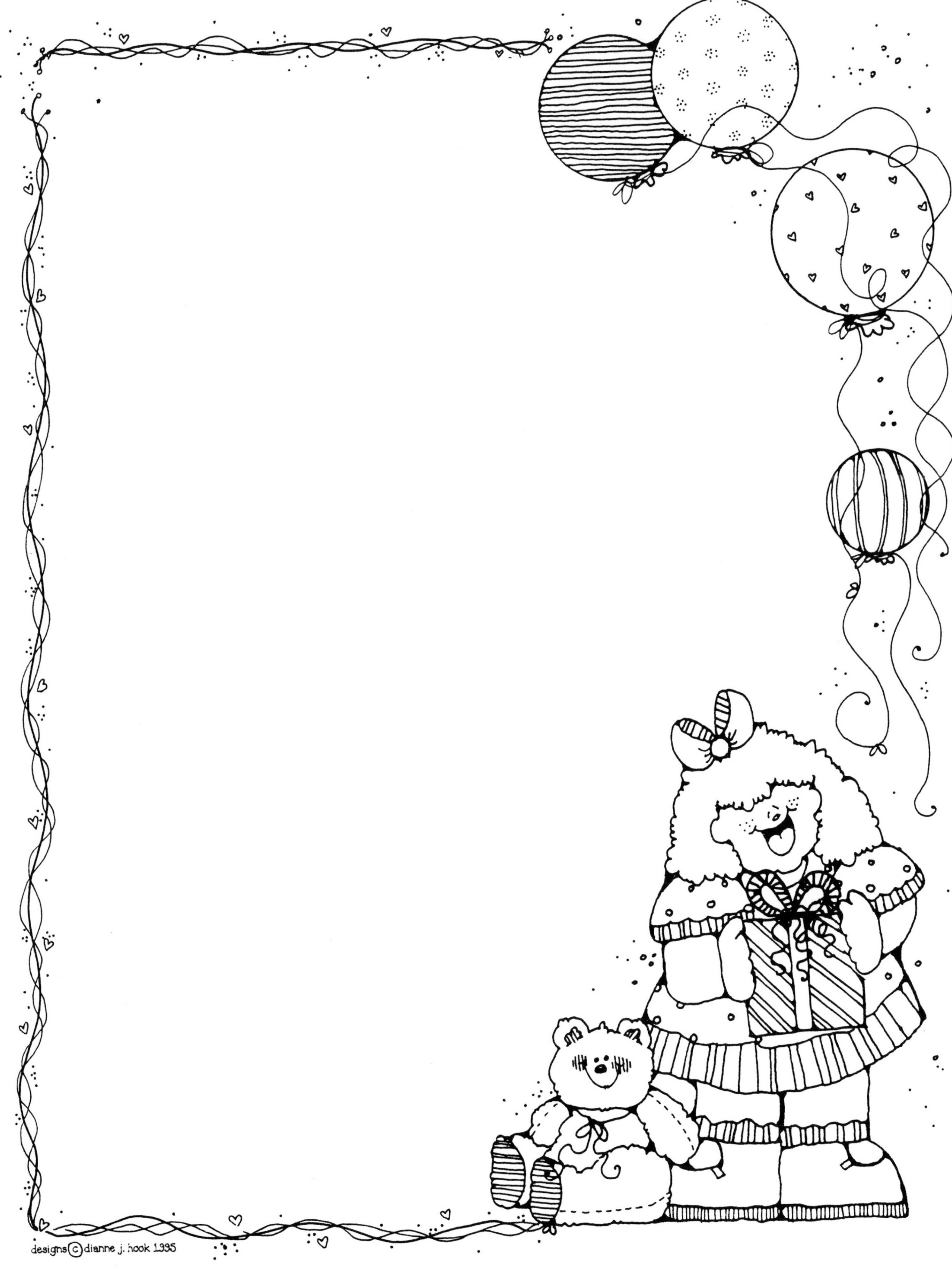
designs © dianne j. hook 1995

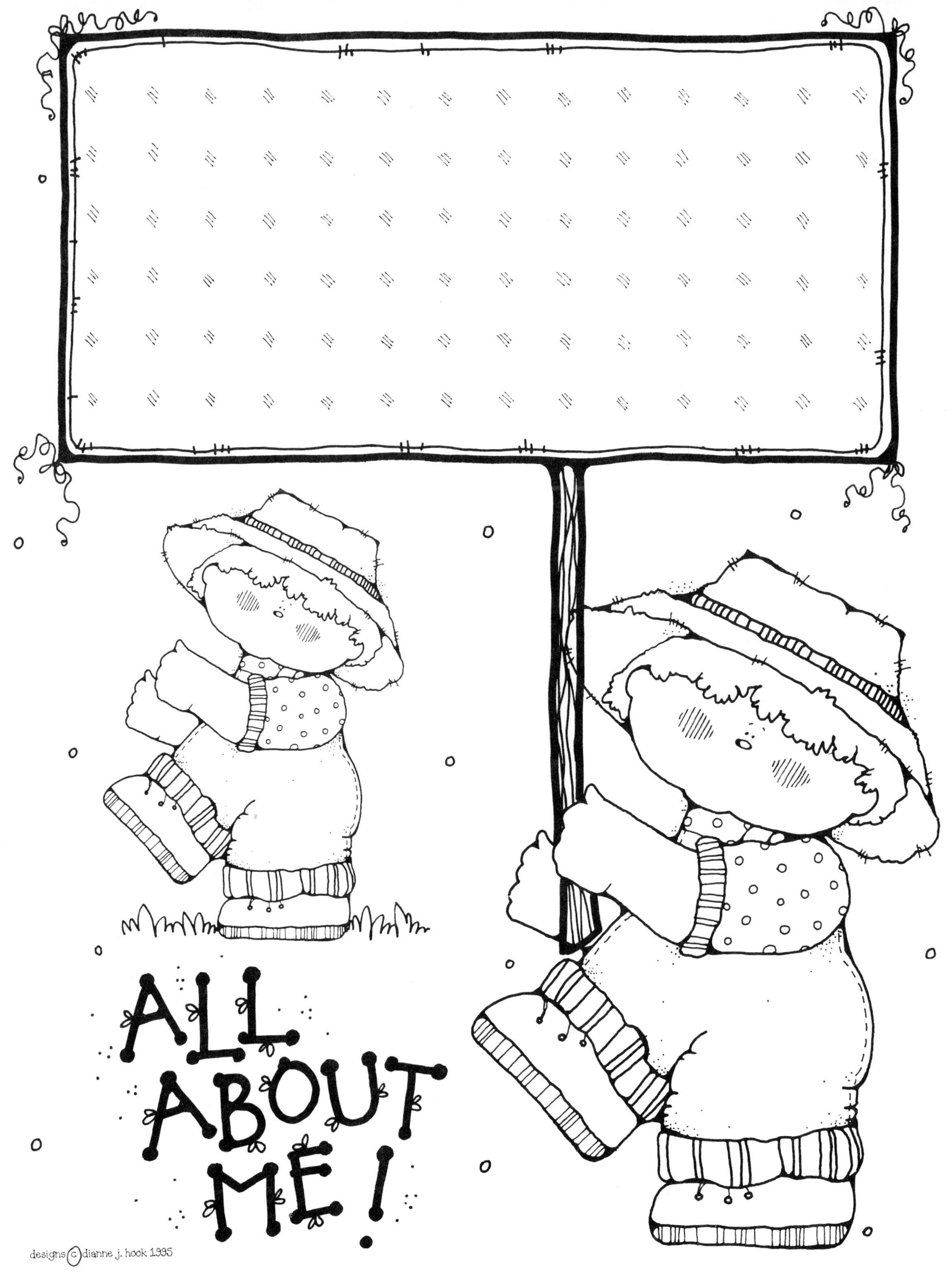

ALL ABOUT ME !
designs (c) dianne j. hook 1995

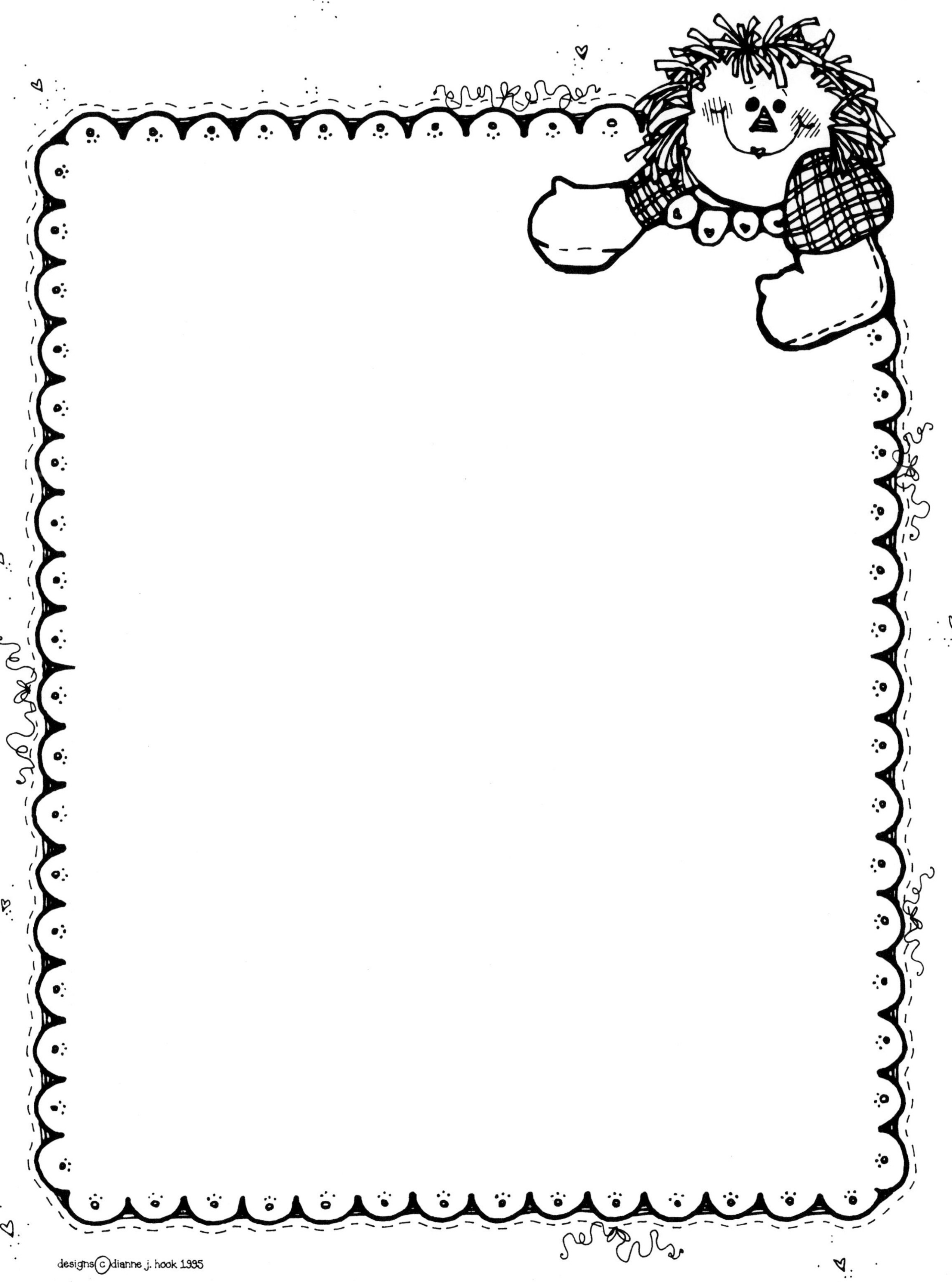

designs © dianne j. hook 1995

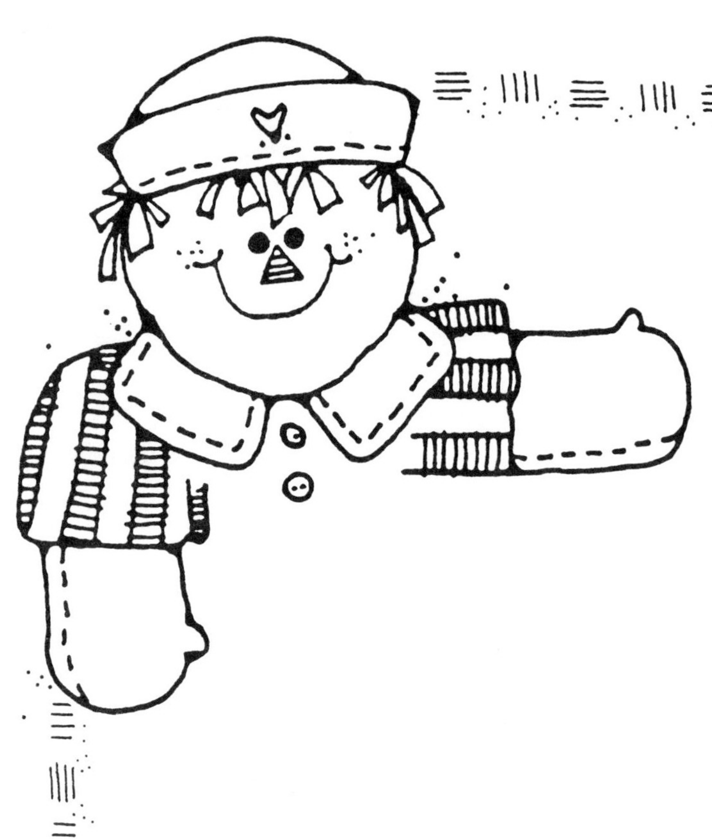
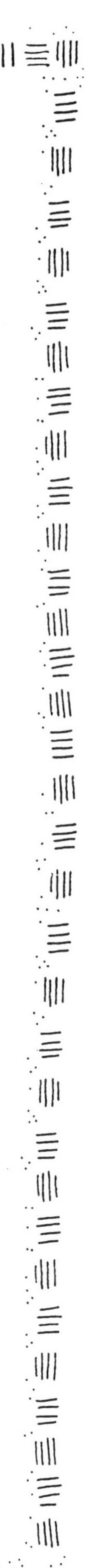

designs © dianne j. hook 1995

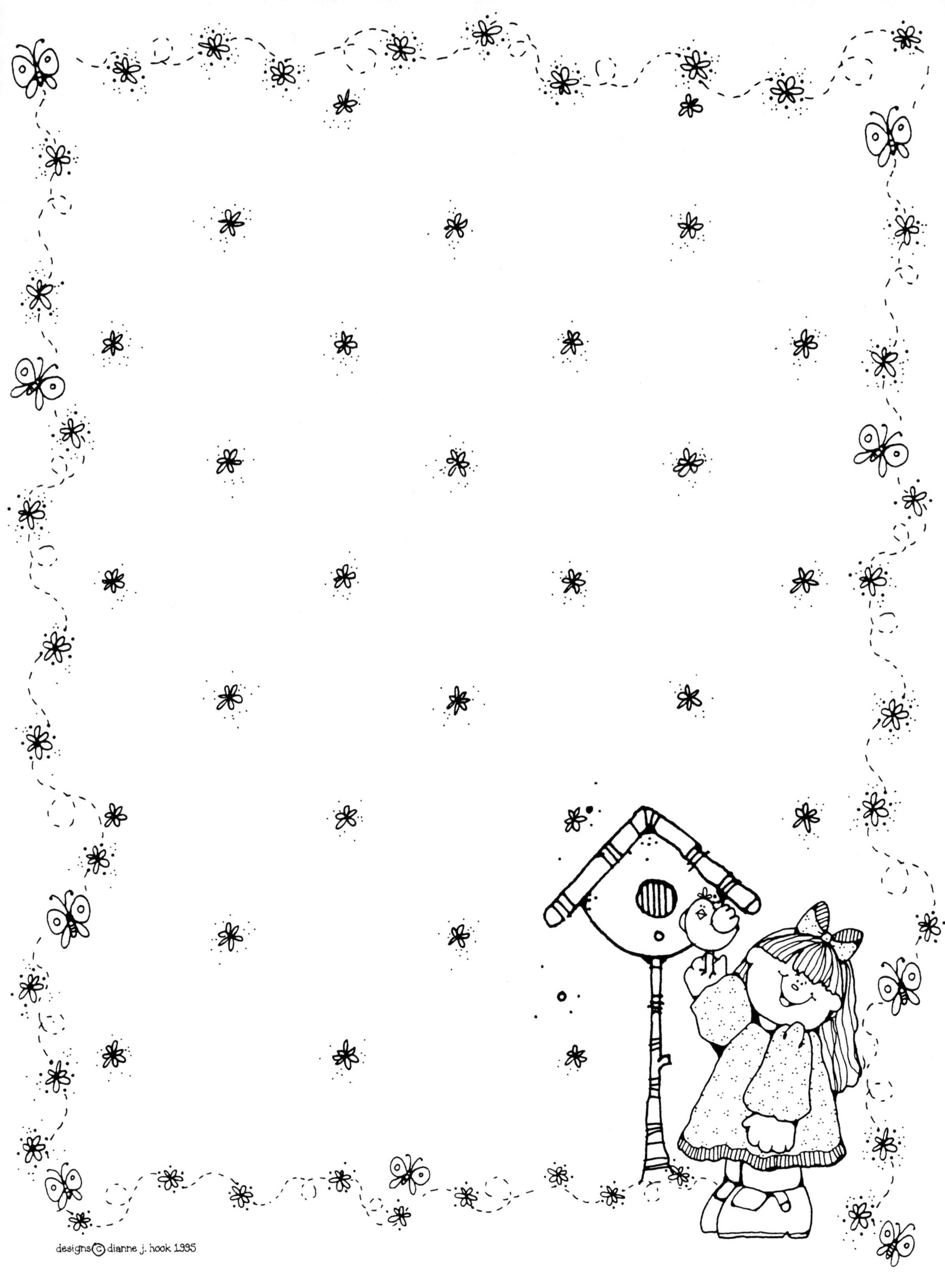

designs © dianne j. hook 1995

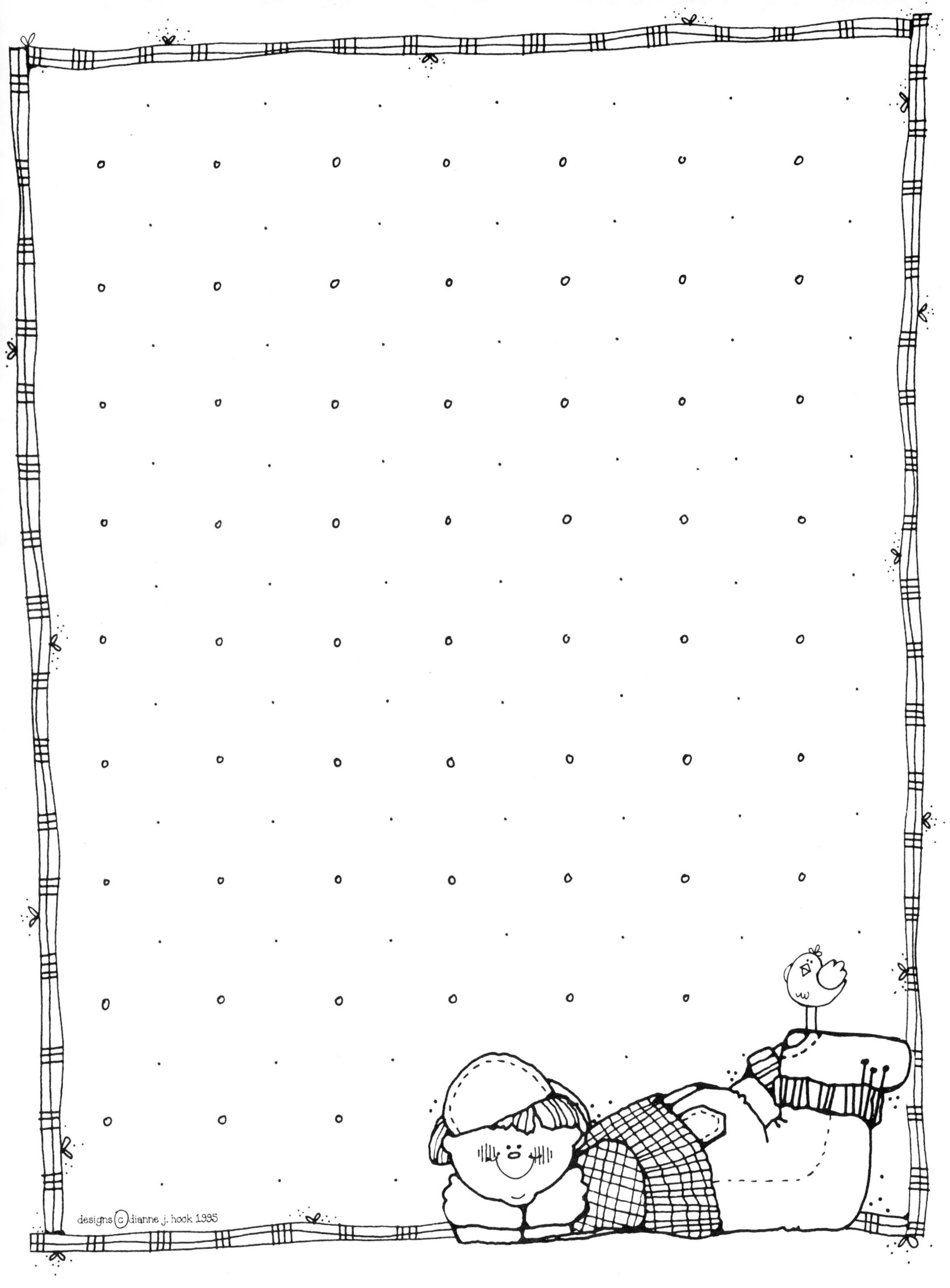

designs © dianne j. hook 1995

Count your many blessings

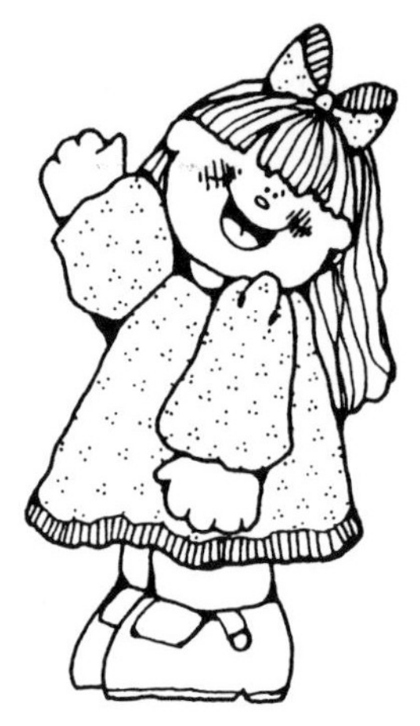

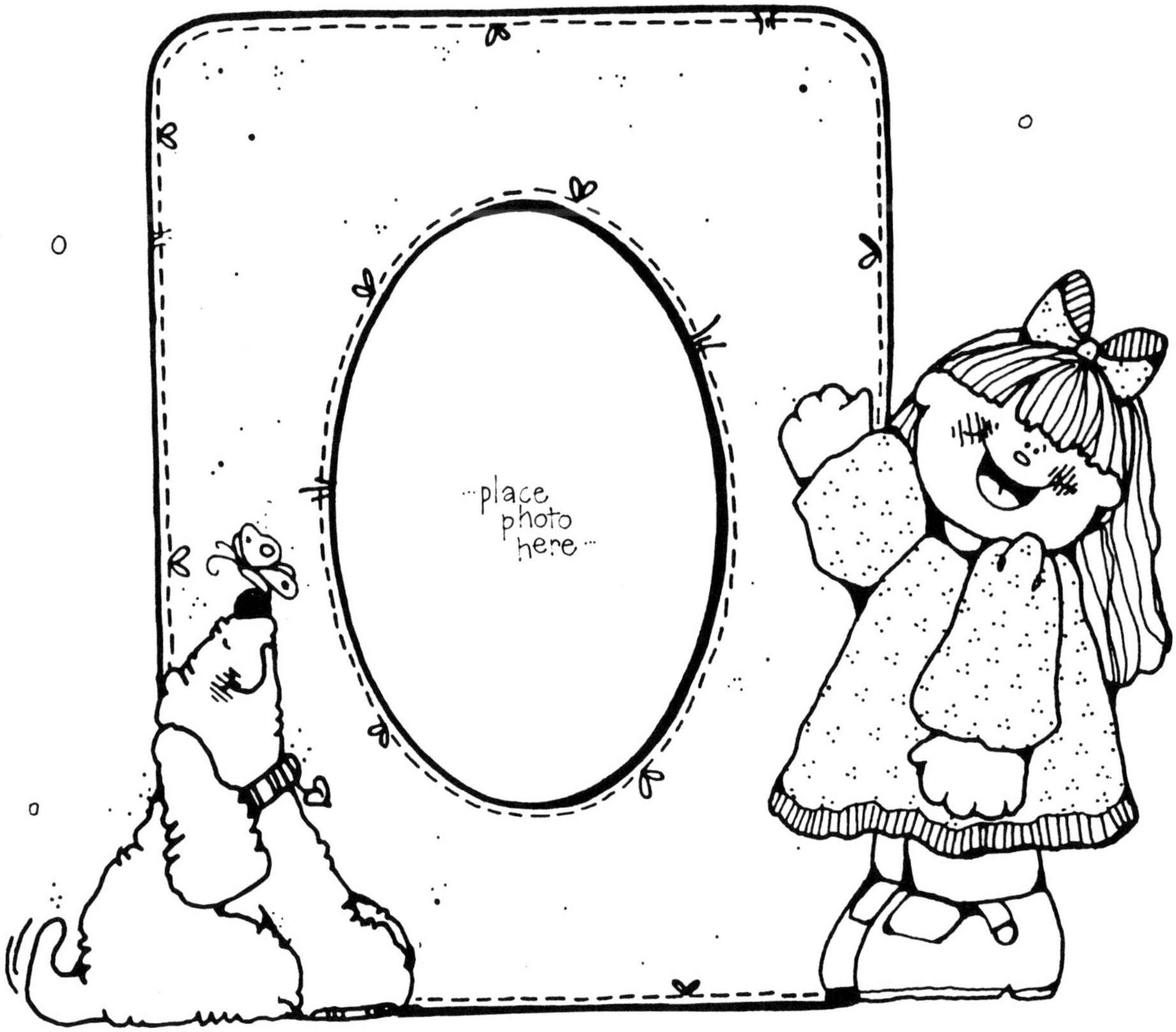

place
photo
here

designs © dianne j. hook 1995

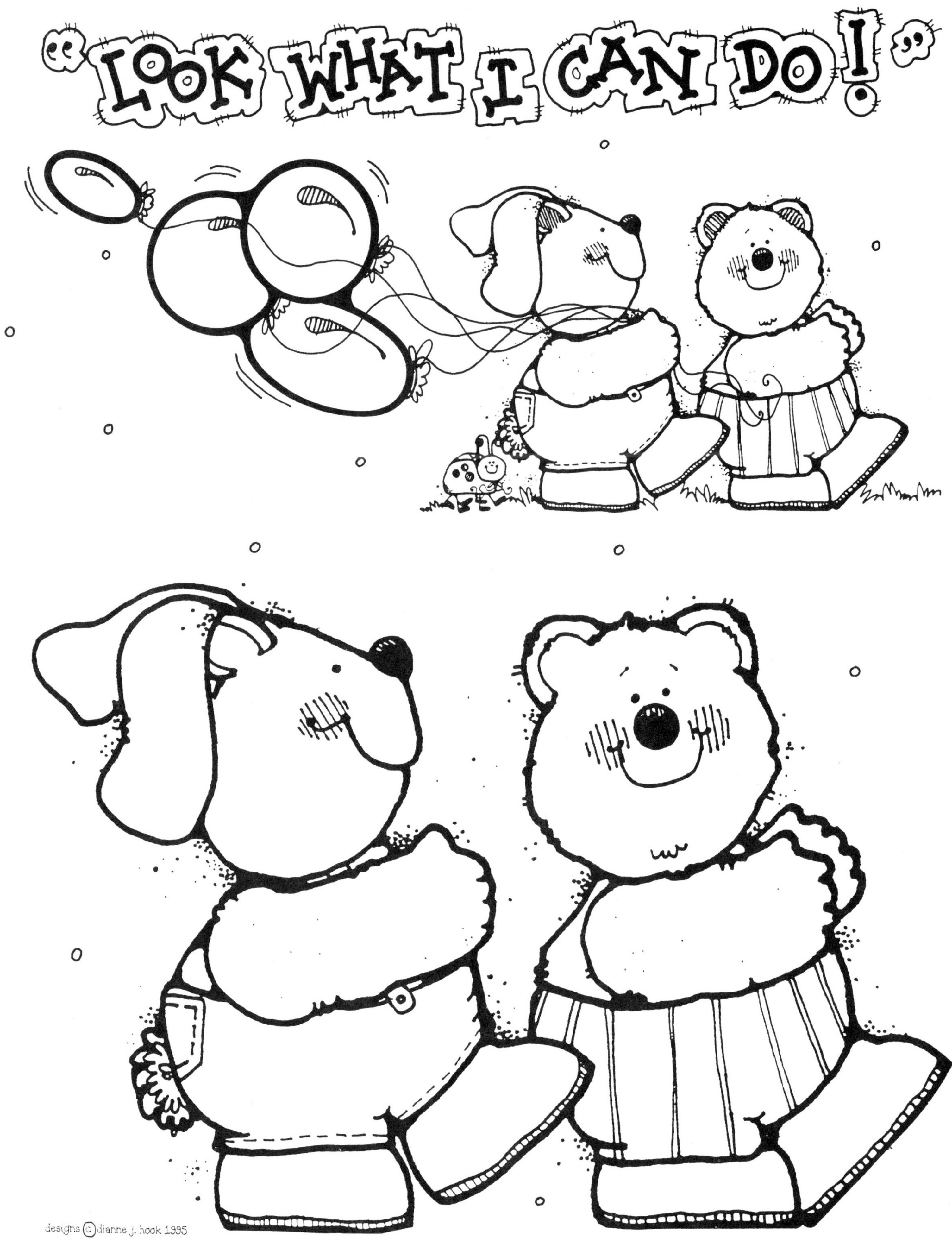

"LOOK WHAT I CAN DO!"
designs © dianne j. hook 1995

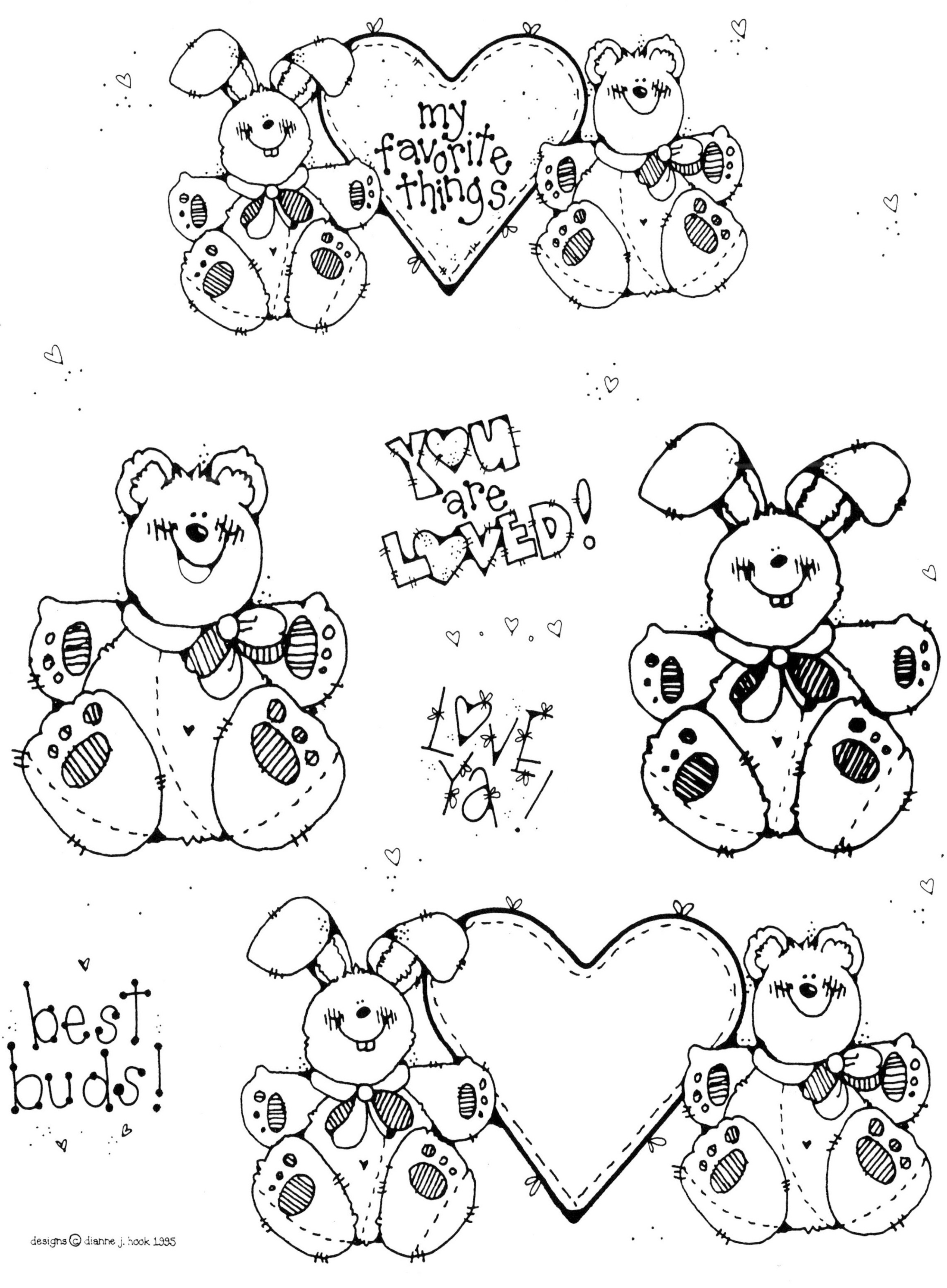

my favorite things
YOU are LOVED!
LOVE YA!
best buds!
designs © dianne j. hook 1995

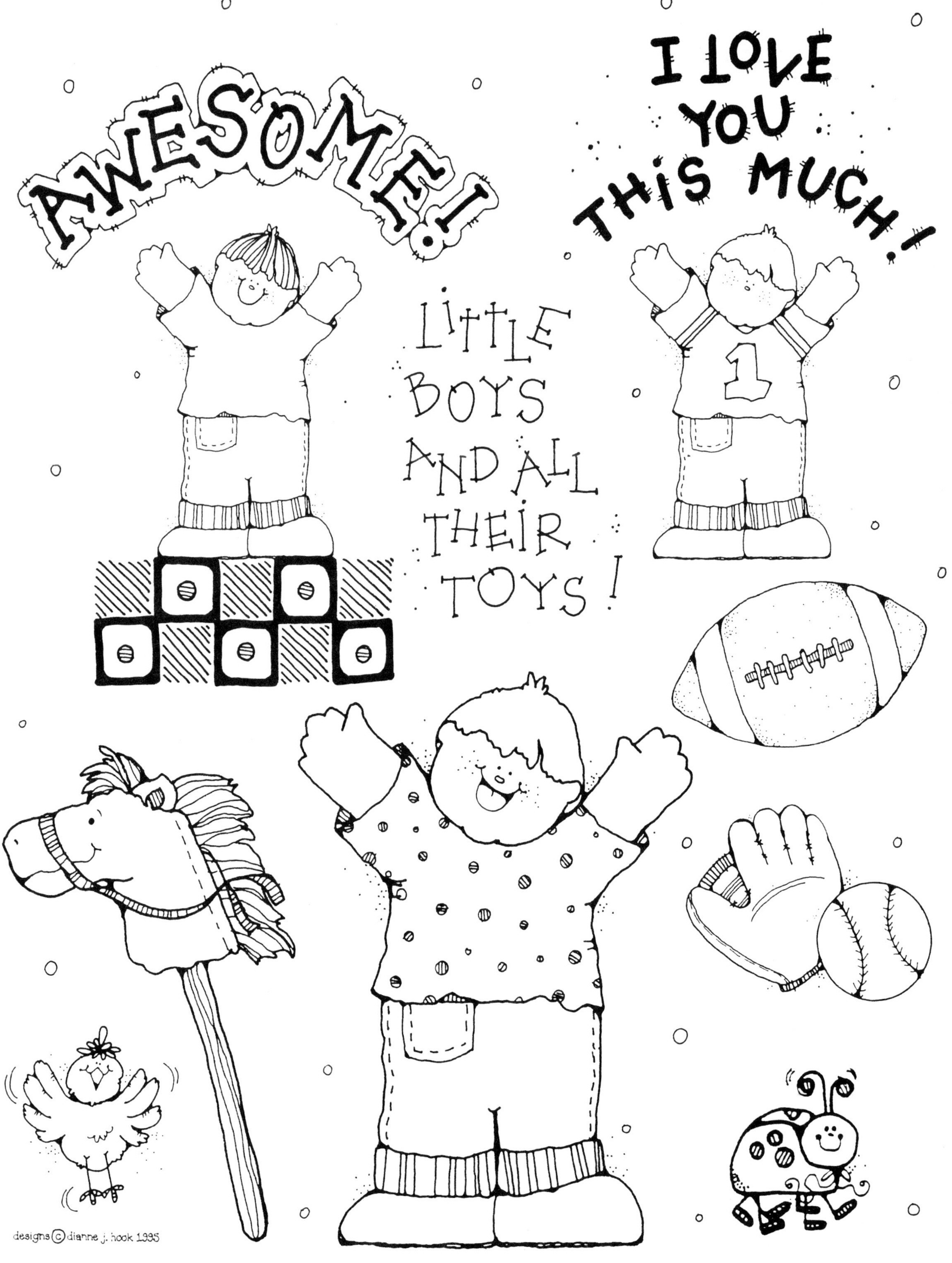

AWESOME!
I LOVE YOU THIS MUCH!
LITTLE BOYS AND ALL THEIR TOYS!
1
designs © dianne j. hook 1995

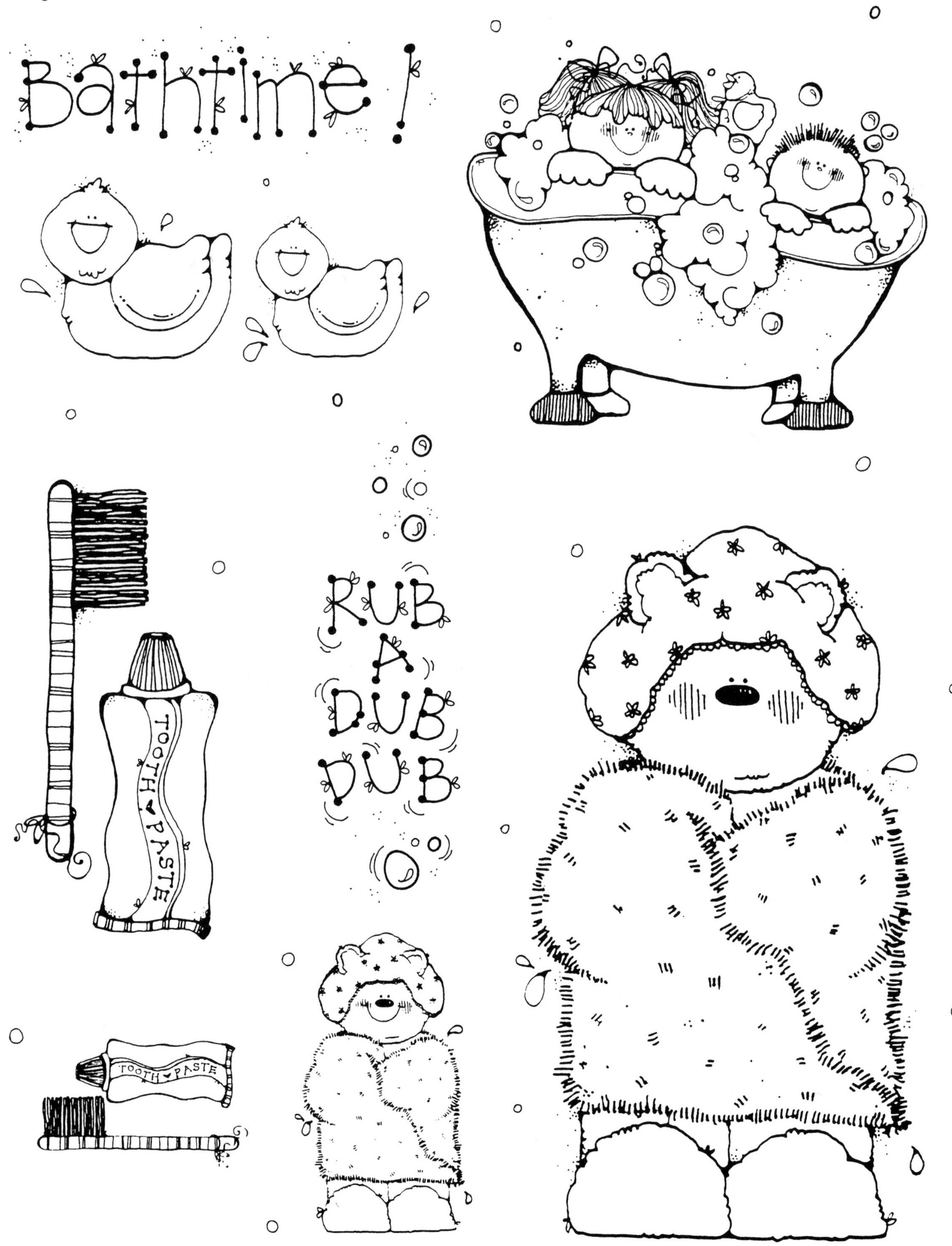

designs © dianne j. hook 1995

little treasures
simple pleasures

heart & home

grandma loves me !

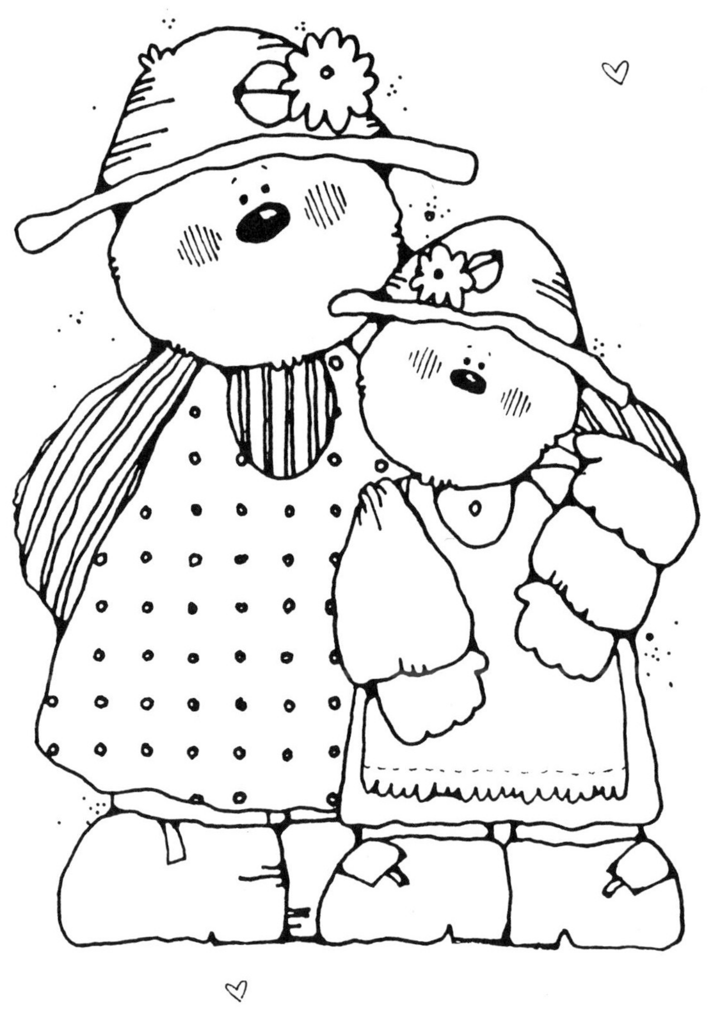

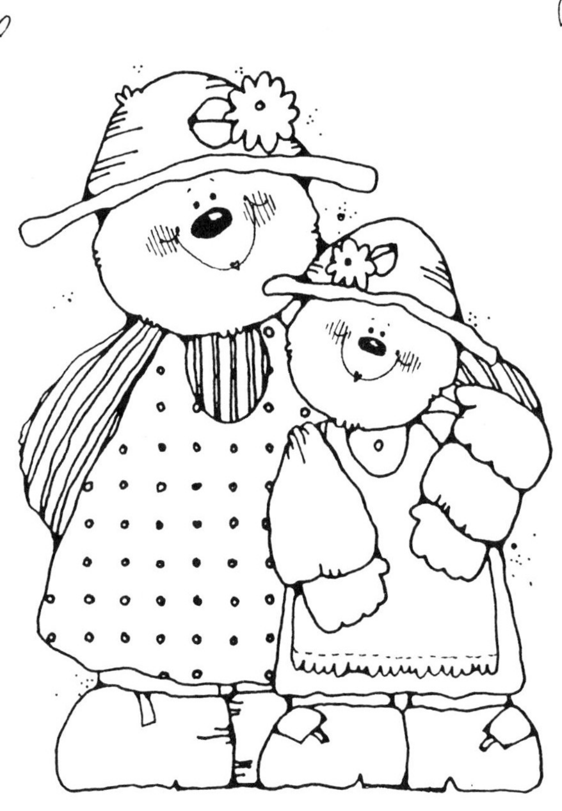

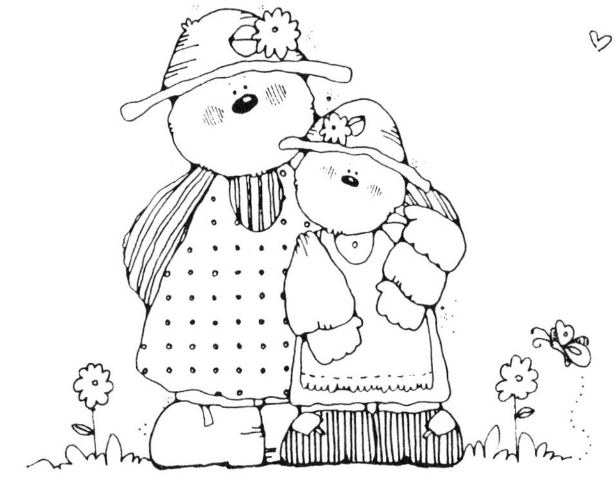

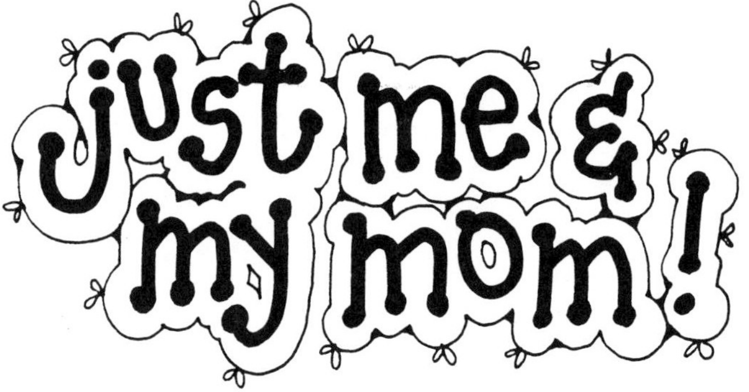

designs © dianne j. hook 1995

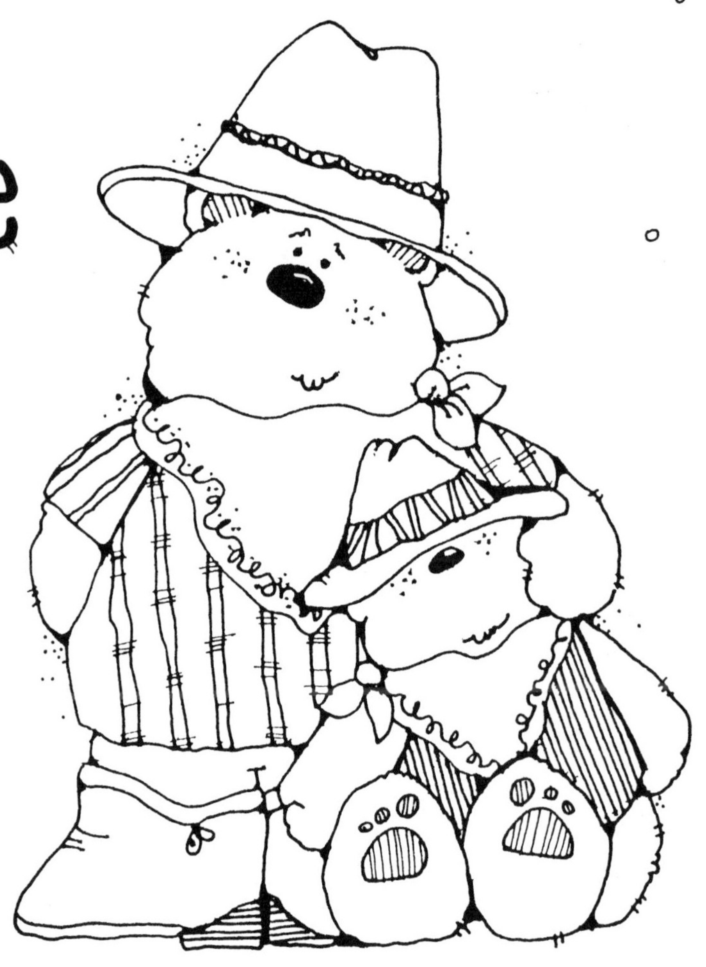

Special people
in my life...

my family...

grandpa
loves me !

Bear Hugs

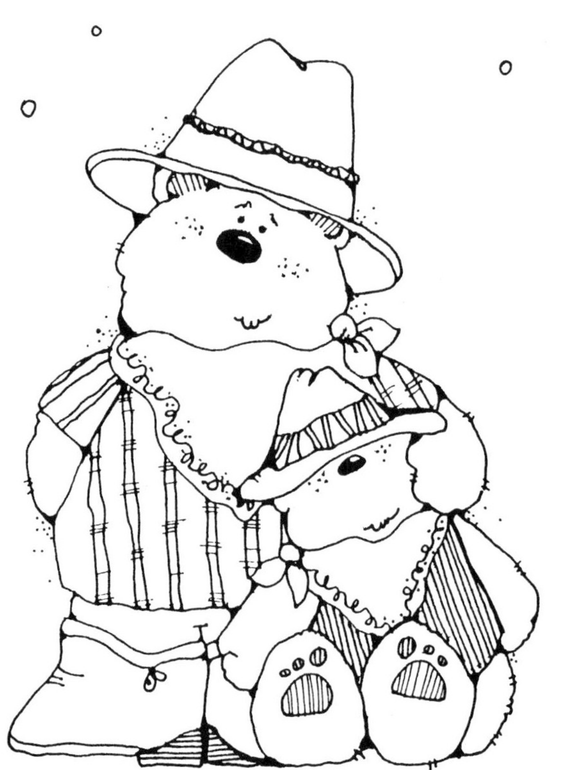

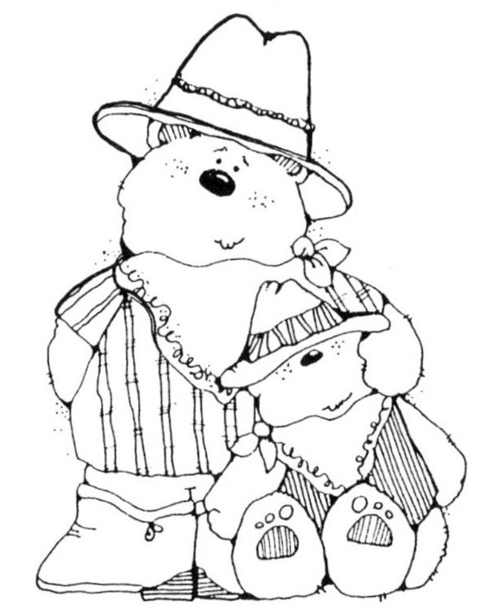

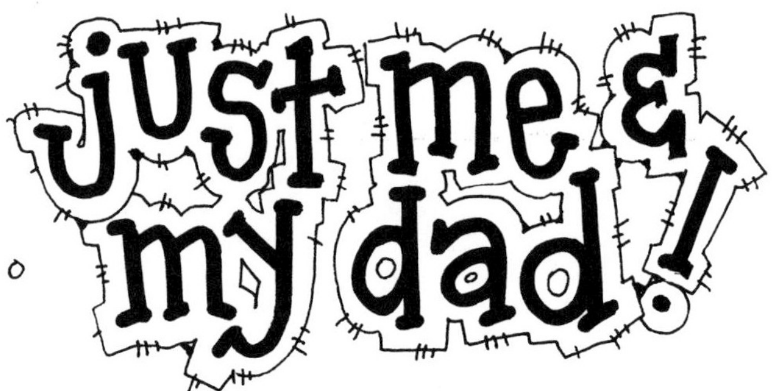

designs © dianne j. hook 1995

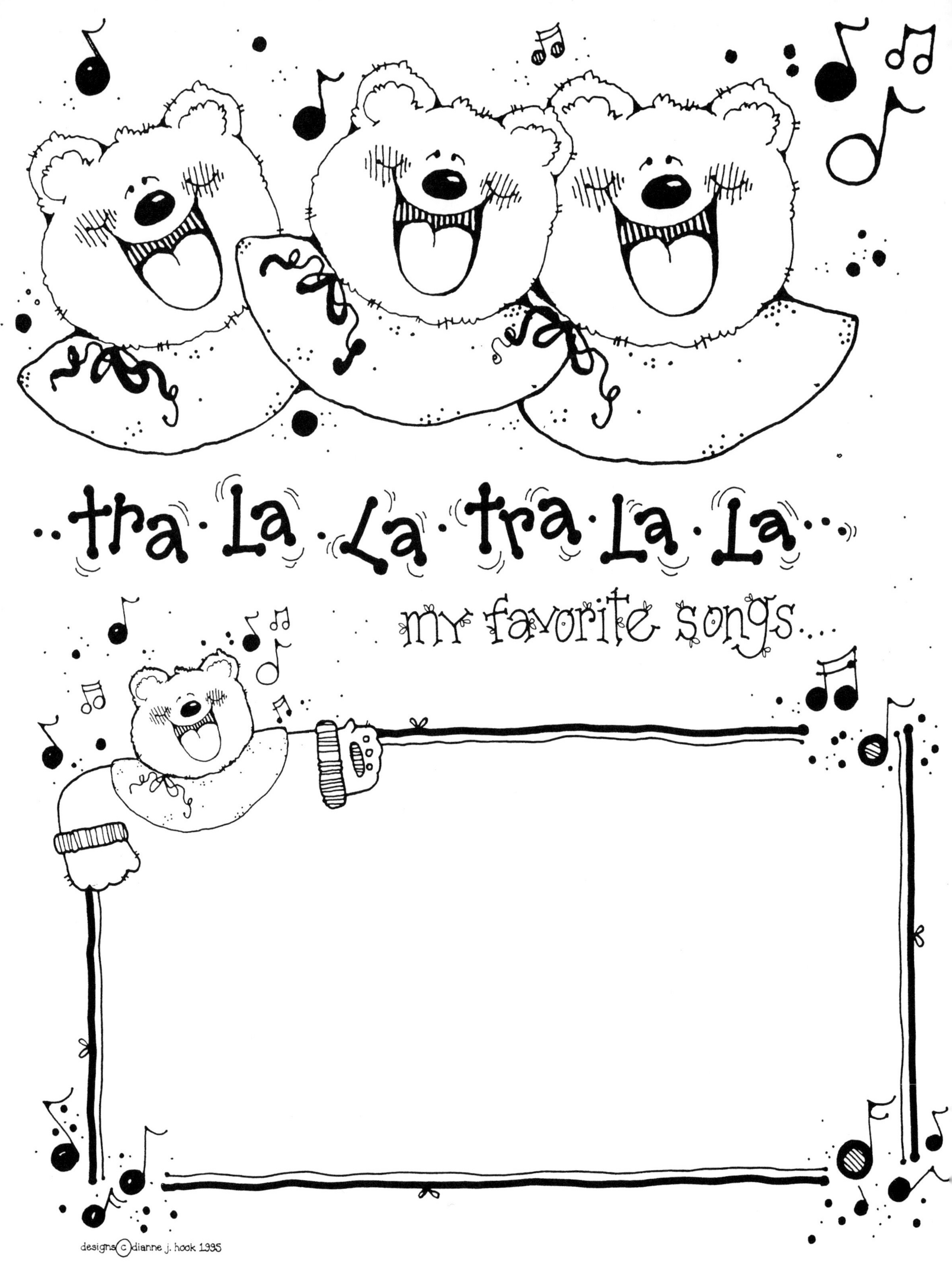

tra La La tra La La
my favorite songs...
designs © dianne j. hook 1995

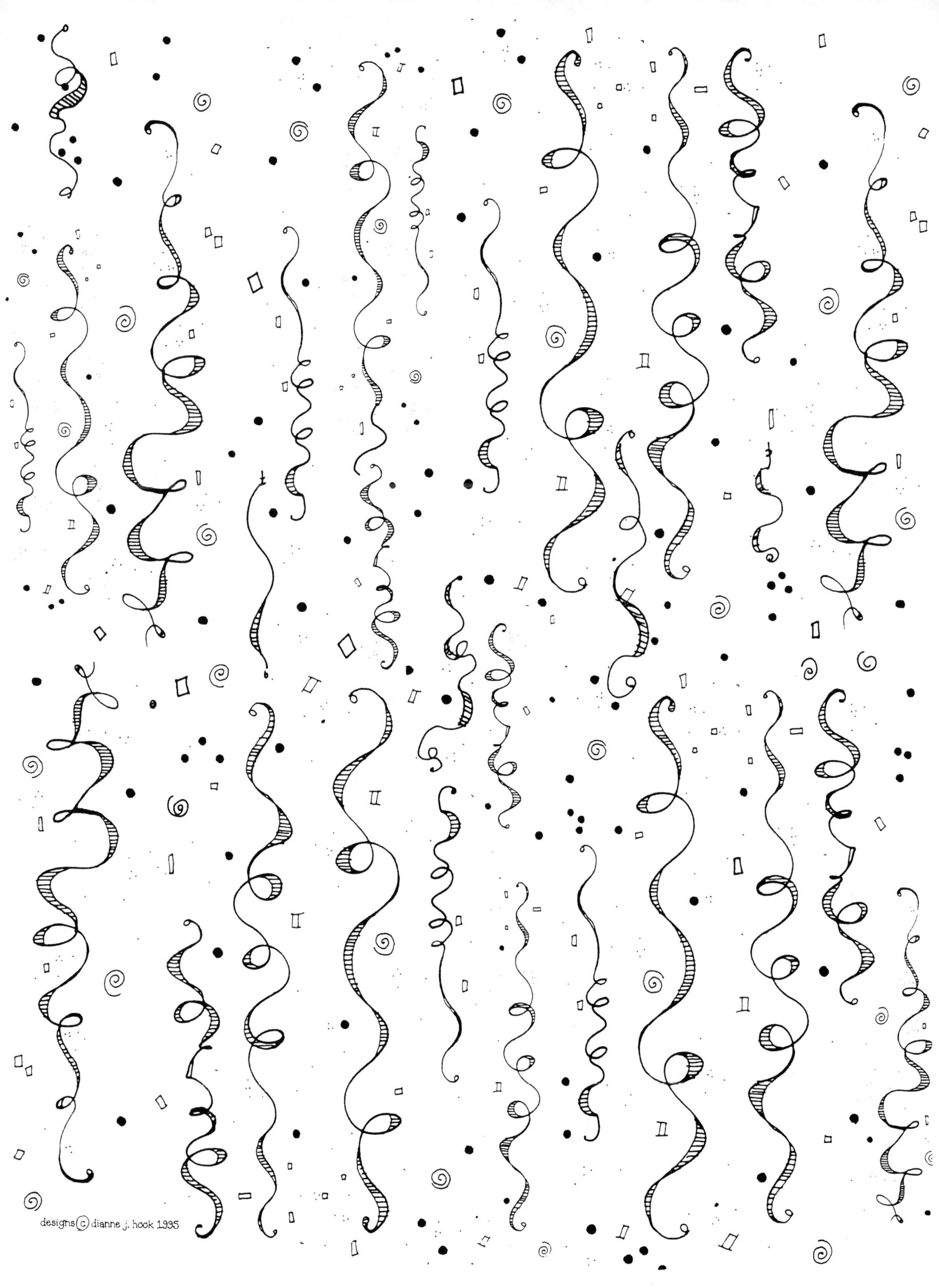
designs © dianne j. hook 1995

designs ©dianne j. hook 1995

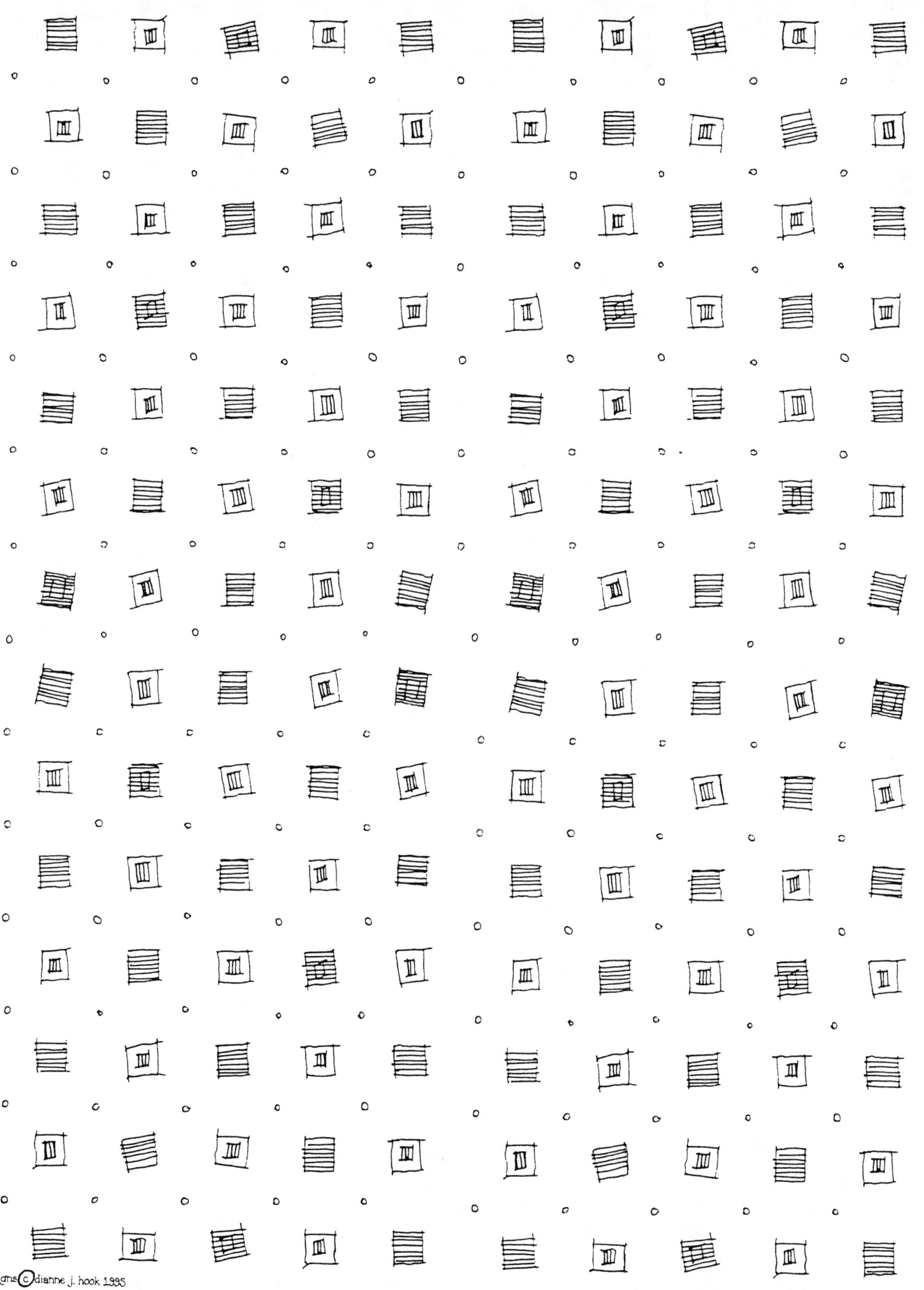

esigns © dianne j. hook 1995

designs © dianne j. hook 1995